Dens and Nests

Anna Harris

Explorer Challenge

What lives in this?

OXFORD
UNIVERSITY PRESS

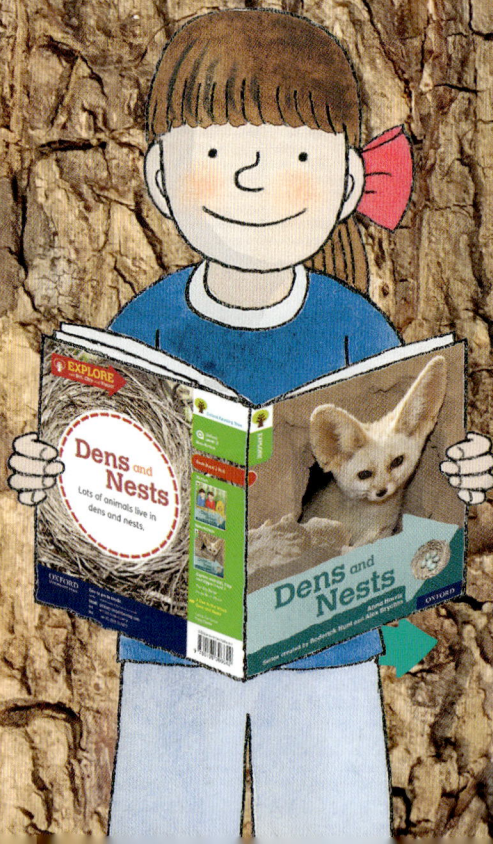

Contents

Ant

I am an ant.

tunnel

ant

eggs

This is an ant nest.

Ants dig tunnels to live in.

Lots of animals live in nests and dens.

5

Redwing

This is a redwing.

Its nest is moss and mud.

eggs

moss

7

Bobcat

This is a bobcat.

Bobcats live in dens in rocks.

kitten

Puffin

This is a puffin.

Puffins dig tunnels.

puffin nest

The nest is in the tunnel.

Fennec Fox

This is a fennec fox.

It digs a den.

den

The fox lives in the den.

Parrot

This is a parrot.

Its nest is in a crack in the tree.

Chimp

This is a chimp.

This chimp is in its nest in a tree.

I am off to *my* nest!

Dens and Nests

Look Back, Explorers

Where was the bobcat's den?

Can you name an animal that has a nest?

Can you think of any words to describe the redwing's eggs?

Did you find out what lives in this?

Explorer Challenge: a puffin (page 11)

19

What's Next, Explorers?

Now join Biff, Chip and Kipper when they spot a den in the wood …

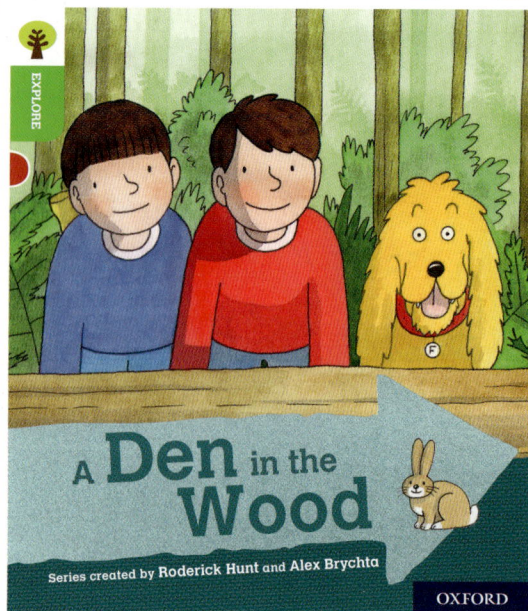

A **Den** in the **Wood**

Series created by Roderick Hunt and Alex Brychta

OXFORD

Explorer Challenge
for *A Den in the Wood*

What lives in this nest?